PRINCIPLES
OF WAR

GENERAL CARL VON CLAUSEWITZ

PRINCIPLES

OF WAR

CARL VON CLAUSEWITZ

Translated and Edited with an Introduction by

Hans W. Gatzke

DOVER PUBLICATIONS, INC.

MINEOLA, NEW YORK

Bibliographical Note

This Dover edition, first published in 2003, is an unabridged reprint of the work published by The Military Service Publishing Company, Harrisburg, Pennsylvania, in 1942.

Library of Congress Cataloging-in-Publication Data

Clausewitz, Carl von, 1780-1831.
    [Wichtigsten Grundsätze des Kriegführens. English]
    Principles of war / Carl von Clausewitz ; translated and edited, with an introduction by Hans W. Gatzke.
        p. cm.
    Originally published: Harrisburg, Pa. : Military Service Pub. Co., 1942.
    ISBN-13: 978-0-486-42799-7 (pbk.)
    ISBN-10: 0-486-42799-4 (pbk.)
    1. Military art and science. 2. Tactics. 3. Strategy. I. Gatzke, Hans Wilhelm, 1915- II. Title.

U102 .C6625 2003
355.02—dc21
                                                                2002035176

Manufactured in the United States by Courier Corporation
42799408   2014
www.doverpublications.com

TABLE OF CONTENTS

INTRODUCTION

Carl von Clausewitz, spiritual father of the German army, has long been recognized as one of the greatest and most original writers on the subject of war. "Only if we understand the nature of warfare in the spirit of Clausewitz can we hope to maintain our existence in case necessity should once again force the sword into our hands." These words introduced to the German army and the German people in 1936 a new edition of Clausewitz' essay, "The Most Important Principles For The Conduct Of War." With equal, if not greater validity, they may serve to introduce the English translation of the same essay.

Clausewitz' life was that of a soldier. It was rarely happy, never easy, and it did not see the fulfillment of his fondest hope: to gain a position of sufficient influence, that he might translate into reality his ideas on the theory and conduct of war.

Born in 1780, a son of a retired Prussian officer, he joined the army when he was only twelve years old. After participating in the War of the First Coalition against France in 1793-94, he spent several trying and uneventful years as officer in the small garrison of Neuruppin. He made use of this period to complete the defective education of his early years, studying in particular the writings of King Frederick II of Prussia, whose character and concept of duty he deeply admired.

In 1801 he entered the "War School" (Kriegsschule), a training school for officers at Berlin. Insufficient preparation as well as financial hardship made life very difficult, adding an element of pessimism to his already overly sensitive character. After a while, however, one of his instructors, the great Scharnhorst, recognized Clausewitz' brilliance and outstanding ability and gave him the encouragement and friendship he needed. As a result Clausewitz became one of his best pupils, and in 1803, on Scharnhorst's recommendation, he became aide-de-camp to Prince August of Prussia. As such he accompanied his royal master in the campaign of 1806 against Napoleon, and was taken prisoner by the French.

After his return to Germany in 1807 he worked in close collaboration with Scharnhorst, whose ideas on military theory and on the necessity of reforming the Prussian army he shared. The influence of Scharnhorst on Clausewitz was profound, and after the death of the great reformer in 1813, Clausewitz considered himself in many respects the intellectual heir of the "father and friend" of his spirit. In 1810, again on Scharnhorst's recommendation, he was attached (as major) to the Prussian General Staff, and was given a position at the "General War School" (Allgemeine Kriegsschule). This school, founded in 1810, was an outgrowth of the earlier schools of officers and eventually developed into the famous "War Academy" (Kriegsakademie). It was at this time that Clausewitz became a close friend of General Gneisenau, who, like Scharnhorst, was one of the leading figures of the Prussian army, and Marshal Blücher's chief of staff in the campaigns against Napoleon. A proof that Clausewitz' ability was recognized is the fact that he was also appointed military instructor of the Prussian crown prince, Frederick William.

These were the years which saw the phenomenal rise of Napoleon. Clausewitz, though a great admirer of Napoleon the soldier, was deeply opposed to Napoleon the conquering dictator. Therefore, when his King, Frederick William III, concluded a treaty with France in 1812, Clausewitz followed the example of many of his fellow-officers and left the service of his country, after publicly and courageously defending his step. On his way to Russia, to join the army of Tsar Alexander I against Napoleon, he completed the memorandum which he had written for the military instruction of his royal pupil, entitled: "The Most Important Principles For The Conduct Of War To Complete My Course Of Instruction Of His Royal Highness The Crown Prince," the translation of which is given in this book.

While in Russia he served as intermediary between Tsar Alexander and the Prussian General Yorck, negotiating the Convention of Tauroggen which eventually brought Prussia back to the side of the powers allied against Napoleon. Clausewitz took part in the Wars of Liberation, first with the Russian army and later as colonel in the army of his own country. Like his friend Scharnhorst, he was never entrusted with the actual conduct of a major military operation, but had to content himself with staff duties. As chief of staff of the third army corps, under General Thielemann, he took part in the Waterloo Campaign, and remained in this position, after peace was concluded, until 1818.

It is doubtful whether Clausewitz would have made a successful leader of armies, considering his reserve and shyness, which gave him the reputation of being cold and conceited. He was too sensitive, too much of the intellectual perhaps, aware of the manifold aspects of a problem, to possess the singleness of purpose which he himself demanded from a military leader. On the other hand, his boundless energy and his sense of reality made him eager to transform into action his thought on things military. The impossibility of doing so accounts for much of his unhappiness and dissatisfaction.

In 1818 he was promoted Major-General and called to Berlin to become head of the Prussian War School, a position which he held until shortly before his death. His duties, unfortunately, were limited to the administration of the school and offered little opportunity for an improvement of the curriculum along the lines of his revolutionary ideas on warfare. Finding himself deprived of all other outlets, Clausewitz turned to writing as the only means of expressing and developing his ideas. It was during this period that he wrote the bulk of his military works, especially his most famous, entitled VOM KRIEGE ("On War").

While still in the midst of his writing, he was made chief of artillery inspection at Breslau, and shortly afterwards chief of staff to Field Marshal Gneisenau's army of observation which had been sent to Posen during the Polish rebellion of 1830. Clausewitz was happy to escape his fruitless administrative duties, but the sudden death of his friend Gneisenau brought new unhappiness. Much overworked, as always, he returned to Germany in 1831. There he came down with a serious attack of cholera, caught during his stay in Posen, and on November 16, 1831, he died, "pushing aside his life like a heavy burden."

The writings of Clausewitz were published only after his death. He had been aware that they constituted "a revolution in the thought of war," and his sensitive nature feared the misunderstanding and immature criticism of his contemporaries. His widow, Marie von Clausewitz, understanding companion and collaborator for twenty years, published the ten volumes of his collected works between 1832 and 1837.

The first three of these, entitled VOM KRIEGE, contain the sum and substance of Clausewitz' thought "On War," and constitute, in the words of Count Schlieffen, "in content and form the greatest work on war ever written." The book is incomplete, and in many of its specific details and illustrations it has been outdated by the tremendous technical developments since Clausewitz' time. Yet, inasmuch as it was not intended to be a specific instruction for the conduct of military operations but rather a philosophical appraisal of war, it possesses a timeless quality which makes it as vital today as ever.

Clausewitz was aware that the French Revolution and its heir, Napoleon, had profoundly affected the character and methods of warfare. War was no longer a careful process of maneuvering for positions with small, expensive armies, trying to reach a decision by the less bloody and costly method of interrupting the enemy's lines of supply. War had become a contest of mass armies in which elements of speed and concentrated, superior effort (forgotten since the days of Frederick the Great) were once again decisive. "Victory is purchased by blood," and complete victory is assured only through destruction of the enemy's forces. Such is Clausewitz' unlimited war of annihilation, his absolute war. "War is an act of violence, pushed to its utmost bounds." This act of violence, moreover, is not divorced from the political life of a nation, it is not an abnormal situation, but merely the forceful realization of a political aim, "a mere continuation of policy by other means." Therefore it must be dictated by political considerations, and military leadership of a state must be subordinated to its political leadership.

Clausewitz' work, in his own words, is the result of "thought and observation, philosophy and experience." To back up his generalizations he refers continually to actual campaigns, many of which he had thoroughly studied and in some of which he had himself participated. But to consider him merely the interpreter of the achievements of others, especially of Napoleon, would be to overlook the originality of his thought as well as the flexibility of his ideas. He was well aware that warfare would again change, as it had done so often in the past.

A large part of Clausewitz' book "On War" is devoted to an evaluation of the moral factors involved in warfare. These sections, in which he treats what might be called the "psychological aspects" of war, have been considered his most unique and enduring contributions. In contrast to the emphasis which 18th century warfare and military theory placed on material forces and mathematical calculations, he stresses the necessity of such intangible qualities as courage, audacity, and self-sacrifice, showing himself perfectly aware of the extreme importance of army morale and public opinion. Exceptional qualities of character, a deep devotion to duty, and a well-rounded personality are the prerequisites of military leadership. They are necessary to overcome the frictions inherent in war and to reach "heroic decisions based on reason," which are the truest expression of superior leadership.

Clausewitz' desire to write a book on war "which would not be forgotten in two or three years" was fulfilled. He wrote a classic which has

made a deep and lasting impression, not only on
the army of his own country, but on that of
other nations as well. (Parts of his writings were
translated into English as early as 1843!) His ideas
were first put into effect by Helmuth von Moltke,
chief of staff of the Prussian army after 1857; and
Prussia's success in the wars of 1866 and 1870-71
was considered proof of the validity of Clausewitz'
teachings. Moltke's second successor, Count
Schlieffen, was likewise a great admirer and dis-
ciple of Clausewitz. Moltke, who had been at the
War School under Clausewitz, recognized that certain adjustments had to be made in the application
of Clausewitz' theories, because of the technical,
social, and economic developments of the Industrial
Revolution. Both he and Schlieffen realized, for
example, that Clausewitz' decision in favor of concentrated frontal attack was no longer feasible, because of the defensive power of modern weapons,
and proposed instead to defeat the enemy by
strategic turning moves (e.g., Schlieffen's famous
Plan of 1905). Such open-minded and broad inter-
pretation of Clausewitz' principles endows them
with lasting significance, no matter how modern
conditions may differ from those during the age
of Napoleon and Clausewitz. In 1937, upon publication of the 15th edition of VOM KRIEGE, the
German Minister of War, General von Blomberg,
wrote: "In spite of all changes of military organization and technique, Clausewitz' book 'On War'

remains for all times the basis for any meaningful development of the art of war."

As appendix to the third volume of VOM KRIEGE, we find the memorandum, mentioned above, written for the military instruction of the Prussian crown prince. Though by no means comparable in scope and significance to the main work, it has nevertheless aroused sufficient interest to be published repeatedly in a separate edition. A French translation appeared toward the end of the last century, when the influence of Clausewitz made itself felt in the French army, notably through Marshal Foch. (Also at this time the French École Supérieure de Guerre was founded on the model of the German Kriegsakademie.) Later, during the First World War, an abbreviated version of the memorandum was published in the United States. The interest shown in the little essay is due to the fact that it contains, in brief form, many of the ideas later expressed in Clausewitz' major work. Like nothing else, therefore, it may serve as an introduction to his theories on the nature and conduct of war. Its brevity, moreover, should not blind us to the vital significance of its contents, which supply enough food for thought "to occupy the whole life of an officer."

The Germans thought enough of the memorandum to republish it in 1936, with an introduction by General Friedrich von Cochenhausen, military writer and instructor at the German Academy for Aerial Warfare. It is significant that a General of

Aviation, which is considered the most modern and revolutionary branch of the armed services, found the memorandum worthy of publication. From this recent edition, considerably more complete than any of the earlier ones (including even the one published in Clausewitz' collected works), the present book has been translated.

Cochenhausen stressed the revolutionary features of Clausewitz' theories, but pointed out that some of his ideas, especially on tactics, are out of date, due to the technical advances of the last century. The sections he thought no longer applicable to modern warfare have been indicated in the German edition by italics, a practice which has been maintained throughout this translation.

But most parts of the little essay still have great current value and "might have been written today." This is true, for example, of the chapter dealing with the influence of terrain on warfare. Still more important and typical is Clausewitz' constant stress on the moral elements of warfare. His language, that of a man who also wrote romantic poetry, may sometimes sound strange to modern ears. But his advice: "Be audacious and cunning in your plans, firm and persevering in their execution, determined to find a glorious end," will never lose its significance.

HANS W. GATZKE

Cambridge, Massachusetts
September 1, 1942

THE MOST IMPORTANT PRINCIPLES
FOR THE CONDUCT OF WAR

These principles, though the result of long thought and continuous study of the history of war, have none the less been drawn up hastily, and thus will not stand severe criticism in regard to form. In addition, only the most important subjects have been picked from a great number, since a certain brevity was necessary. These principles, therefore, will not so much give complete instruction to Your Royal Highness, as they will stimulate and serve as a guide for your own reflections.

CARL VON CLAUSEWITZ

I. PRINCIPLES FOR WAR IN GENERAL

1. The theory of warfare tries to discover how we may gain a preponderance of physical forces and material advantages at the decisive point. As this is not always possible, theory also teaches us to calculate moral factors: the likely mistakes of the enemy, the impression created by a daring action, . . . yes, even our own desperation. None of these things lie outside the realm of the theory and art of war, which is nothing but the result of reasonable reflection on all the possible situations encountered during a war. We should think very frequently of the most dangerous of these situations and familiarize ourselves with it. Only thus shall we reach heroic decisions based on reason, which no critic can ever shake.

Any person who may present this matter differently to Your Royal Highness is a pedant, whose views will only be harmful to you. In the decisive moments of your life, in the turmoil of battle, you will some day feel that this view alone can help where help is needed most, and where a dry pedantry of figures will forsake you.

2. Whether counting on physical or moral advantages, we should always try, in time of war, to have the probability of victory on our side. But this is not always possible. Often we must act AGAINST this probability, SHOULD THERE BE NOTHING BETTER TO DO. Were we to despair here, we would abandon the use of reason just when it be-

comes most necessary, when everything seems to be conspiring against us.

Therefore, even when the likelihood of success is against us, we must not think of our undertaking as unreasonable or impossible; for it is always reasonable, if we do not know of anything better to do, and if we make the best use of the few means at our disposal.

We must never lack the calmness and firmness, which are so hard to preserve in time of war. Without them the most brilliant qualities of mind are wasted. We must therefore familiarize ourselves with the thought of an honorable defeat. We must always nourish this thought within ourselves, and we must get completely used to it. Be convinced, Most Gracious Master, that without this firm resolution no great results can be achieved in the most successful war, let alone in the most unsuccessful.

Certainly this thought frequently occupied the mind of Frederick II during his first Silesian wars. Because he was familiar with it he undertook his attack near Leuthen, on that memorable fifth of December, and not because he believed that his oblique formation would very likely beat the Austrians.[1]

3. In any specific action, in any measure we may undertake, we always have the choice between the most audacious and the most careful solution. Some people think that the theory of war always

---

[1] See notes beginning on page 70.

advises the latter. That assumption is false. If the theory does advise anything, it is the nature of war to advise the most decisive, that is, the most audacious. Theory leaves it to the military leader, however, to act according to his own courage, according to his spirit of enterprise, and his self-confidence. Make your choice, therefore, according to this inner force; but never forget that no military leader has ever become great without audacity.

II. TACTICS OR THE THEORY OF COMBAT

War is a combination of many distinct engagements. Such a combination may or may not be reasonable, and success depends very much on this. Yet the engagement itself is for the moment more important. For only a combination of successful engagements can lead to good results. The most important thing in war will always be the art of defeating our opponent in combat. To this matter Your Royal Highness can never turn enough attention and thought. I think the following principles the most important:

1. General Principles For Defense

1. To keep our troops covered as long as possible. Since we are always open to attack, except when we ourselves are attacking, we must at every instant be on the defensive and thus should place our forces as much under cover as possible.

2. Not to bring all our troops into combat immediately. With such action all wisdom in conducting a battle disappears. It is only with troops left at our disposal that we can turn the tide of battle.

3. To be little or not at all concerned about the extent of our front. This in itself is unimportant, and an extension of the front limits the depth of our formation (that is the number of corps which are lined up one behind the other). Troops which

15

are kept in the rear are always available. We can use them either to renew combat at the same point, or to carry the fight to other neighboring points. This principle is a corollary of the previous one.

4. The enemy, while attacking one section of the front, often seeks to outflank and envelop us at the same time. The army-corps [2] which are kept in the background can meet this attempt and thus make up for the support usually derived from obstacles in the terrain. They are better suited for this than if they were standing in line and extending the front. For in this case the enemy could easily outflank them. This principle again is a closer definition of the second.

5. If we have many troops to hold in reserve, only part of them should stand directly behind the front. The rest we should put obliquely behind.

From this position they in turn can attack the flank of the enemy columns which are seeking to envelop us.

6. A fundamental principle is never to remain completely passive, but to attack the enemy frontally and from the flanks, even while he is attacking us. We should, therefore, defend ourselves on a given front merely to induce the enemy to deploy his forces in an attack on this front. Then we in turn attack with those of our troops which we have kept back. The art of entrenchment, as Your Royal Highness expressed so excellently at one time, shall serve the defender not to defend

himself more securely behind a rampart, but to attack the enemy more successfully. This idea should be applied to any passive defense. Such defense is nothing more than a means by which to attack the enemy most advantageously, in a terrain chosen in advance, where we have drawn up our troops and have arranged things to our advantage.

7. This attack from a defensive position can take place the moment the enemy actually attacks, or while he is still on the march. I can also, at the moment the attack is about to be delivered, withdraw my troops, luring the enemy into unknown territory and attacking him from all sides. The formation in depth—*i.e.*, the formation in which only two-thirds or half or still less of the army is drawn-up in front and the rest directly or obliquely behind and hidden, if possible—is very suitable for all these moves. This type of formation is, therefore, of immense importance.

8. If, for example, I had two divisions, I would prefer to keep one in the rear. If I had three, I would keep at least one in the rear, and if four probably two. If I had five, I should hold at least two in reserve and in many cases even three, etc.

9. At those points where we remain passive we must make use of the art of fortification. This should be done with many independent works, completely closed and with very strong profiles.

10. In our plan of battle we must set this great aim: the attack on a large enemy column and its

complete destruction. If our aim is low, while that of the enemy is high, we will naturally get the worst of it. We are penny-wise and pound-foolish.

11. Having set a high goal in our plan of defense (the annihilation of an enemy column, etc.), we must pursue this goal with the greatest energy and with the last ounce of our strength. In most cases the aggressor will pursue his own aim at some other point. While we fall upon his right wing, for example, he will try to win decisive advantages with his left. Consequently, if we should slacken before the enemy does, if we should pursue our aim with less energy than he does, he will gain his advantage completely, while we shall only half gain our's. He will thus achieve preponderance of power; the victory will be his, and we shall have to give up even our partly gained advantages. If Your Royal Highness will read with attention the history of the battles of Ratisbon and Wagram, all this will seem true and important.[3]

In both these battles the Emperor Napoleon attacked with his right wing and tried to hold out with his left. The Archduke Charles did exactly the same. But, while the former acted with great determination and energy, the latter was wavering and always stopped half-way. That is why the advantages which Charles gained with the victorious part of his army were without consequence, while those which Napoleon gained at the opposite end were decisive.

12. Let me sum up once more the last two principles. Their combination gives us a maxim which should take first place among all causes of victory in the modern art of war: "Pursue one great decisive aim with force and determination."

13. If we follow this and fail, the danger will be even greater, it is true. But to increase caution at the expense of the final goal is no military art. It is the wrong kind of caution, which, as I have said already in my "General Principles," is contrary to the nature of war. For great aims we must dare great things. When we are engaged in a daring enterprise, the right caution consists in not neglecting out of laziness, indolence, or carelessness those measures which help us to gain our aim. Such was the case of Napoleon, who never, because of caution, pursued great aims in a timid or half-hearted way.

If you remember, Most Gracious Master, the few defensive battles that have ever been won, you will find that the best of them have been conducted in the spirit of the principles voiced here. For it is the study of the history of war which has given us these principles.

At Minden, Duke Ferdinand suddenly appeared where the enemy did not expect him and took the offensive, while at Tannhausen he defended himself passively behind earthworks.[4] At Rossbach Frederick II threw himself against the enemy at an unexpected point and an unexpected moment.[5]

At Liegnitz the Austrians found the King at night in a position very different from that in which they had seen him the previous day. He fell with his whole army upon one enemy column and defeated it before the others could start fighting.[6]

At Hohenlinden Moreau had five divisions in his frontline and four directly behind and on his flanks. He outflanked the enemy and fell upon his right wing before it could attack.[7]

At Ratisbon Marshal Davout defended himself passively, while Napoleon attacked the fifth and sixth army-corps with his right wing and beat them completely.

Though the Austrians were the real defenders at Wagram, they did attack the emperor on the second day with the greater part of their forces. Therefore Napoleon can also be considered a defender. With his right wing he attacked, outflanked and defeated the Austrian left wing. At the same time he paid little attention to his weak left wing (consisting of a single division), which was resting on the Danube. Yet through strong reserves (i.e., formation in depth), he prevented the victory of the Austrian right wing from having any influence on his own victory gained on the Russbach. He used these reserves to retake Aderklaa.

Not all the principles mentioned earlier are clearly contained in each of these battles, but all are examples of active defense.

The mobility of the Prussian army under Frederick II was a means towards victory on which we can no longer count, since the other armies are at least as mobile as we are. On the other hand, outflanking was less common at that time and formation in depth, therefore, less imperative.

2. General Principles For Offense

1. We must select for our attack one point of the enemy's position (*i.e.*, one section of his troops —a division, a corps) and attack it with great superiority, leaving the rest of his army in uncertainty but keeping it occupied. This is the only way that we can use an equal or smaller force to fight with advantage and thus with a chance of success. The weaker we are, the fewer troops we should use to keep the enemy occupied at unimportant points, in order to be as strong as possible at the decisive point. Frederick II doubtlessly won the battle of Leuthen only because he massed his small army together in one place and thus was very concentrated, as compared to the enemy.[8]

2. We should direct our main thrust against an enemy wing by attacking it from the front and from the flank, or by turning it completely and attacking it from the rear. Only when we cut off the enemy's line of retreat are we assured of great success in victory.

3. Even though we are strong, we should still direct our main attack against one point only. In

that way we shall gain more strength at this point. For to surround an army completely is possible only in rare cases and requires tremendous physical or moral superiority. It is possible, however, to cut off the enemy's line of retreat at one point of his flank and thereby already gain great success.

4. Generally speaking, the chief aim is the certainty (high probability) of victory, that is, the certainty of driving the enemy from the field of battle. The plan of battle must be directed towards this end. For it is easy to change an indecisive victory into a decisive one through energetic pursuit of the enemy.

5. Let us assume that the enemy has troops enough on one wing to make a front in all directions. Our main force should try to attack the wing concentrically, so his troops find themselves assailed from all sides. Under these circumstances his troops will get discouraged much more quickly; they suffer more, get disordered—in short, we can hope to turn them to flight much more easily.

6. This encirclement of the enemy necessitates a greater deployment of forces in the front line for the aggressor than for the defender.

If the corps *a b c* should make a concentric attack on the section *e* of the enemy army, they should, of course, be next to each other. But we should never have so many forces in the front line that we have none in reserve. That would be a very great error which would lead to defeat, should the enemy be in the least prepared for an encirclement.

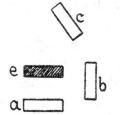

If *a b c* are the corps which are to attack section *e*, the corps *f g* must be held in reserve. With this formation in depth we are able to harass the same point continuously. And in case our troops should be beaten at the opposite end of the line, we do not need to give up immediately our attack at this end, since we still have reserves with which

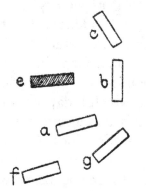

to oppose the enemy. The French did this in the battle of Wagram. Their left wing, which opposed the Austrian right wing resting on the Danube, was extremely weak and was completely defeated. Even their center at Aderklaa was not very strong and was forced by the Austrians to retreat on the first day of battle. But all this did not matter, since Napoleon had such depth on his right wing, with which he attacked the Austrian left from the front and side, that he advanced against the Austrians at Aderklaa with a tremendous column of cavalry and horse-artillery; and, though he could not beat them, he at least was able to hold them there.

7. Just as on the defensive, we should choose as object of our offensive that section of the enemy's army whose defeat will give us decisive advantages.

8. As in defense, as long as any resources are left, we must not give up until our purpose has been reached. Should the defender likewise be active, should he attack us at other points, we shall be able to gain victory only if we surpass him in energy and boldness. On the other hand, should he be passive, we really run no great danger.

9. Long and unbroken lines of troops should be avoided completely. They would lead only to parallel attacks, which today are no longer feasible.

Each division makes its attack separately, though according to the directions of a higher command and thus in agreement with each other. Yet one division (8,000 to 10,000 men) is never formed into one single line, but into two, three, or even four. From this it follows that a long unbroken line is no longer possible.

10. The concerted attacks of the divisions and army corps should not be obtained by trying to

direct them from a central point, so that they
maintain contact and even align themselves on each
other, though they may be far apart or even separated by the enemy. This is a faulty method of
bringing about cooperation, open to a thousand
mischances. Nothing great can be achieved with
it and we are certain to be thoroughly beaten by
a strong opponent.

The true method consists in giving each commander of an army corps or a division the main
direction of his march, and in pointing out the
enemy as the objective and victory as the goal.

Each commander of a column, therefore, has
the order to attack the enemy wherever he may
find him and to do so with all his strength. He
must not be made responsible for the success of
his attack, for that would lead to indecision. But
he is responsible for seeing that his corps will take
part in battle with all its energy and with a spirit
of self-sacrifice.

11. A well-organized, independent corps can
withstand the best attack for some time (several
hours) and thus can not be annihilated in a moment. Thus, even if it engaged the enemy pre-
maturely and was defeated, its fight will not have
been in vain. The enemy will unfold and expend
his strength against this one corps, offering the rest
a good chance for an attack.

The way in which a corps should be organized
for this purpose will be treated later.

We therefore assure the cooperation of all forces by giving each corps a certain amount of independence, but seeing to it that each seeks out the enemy and attacks him with all possible self-sacrifice.

12. One of the strongest weapons of offensive warfare is the surprise attack. The closer we come to it, the more fortunate we shall be. The unexpected element which the defender creates through secret preparations and through the concealed disposition of his troops, can be counterbalanced on the part of the aggressor only by a surprise attack.

Such action, however, has been very rare in recent wars, partly because of the more advanced precautionary measures, partly because of the rapid conduct of campaigns. There seldom arises a long suspension of activities, which lulls one side into security and thus gives the other an opportunity to attack unexpectedly.

Under these circumstances—except for nightly assaults which are always possible (as at Hochkirch)[9]—we can surprise our opponent only by marching to the side or to the rear and then suddenly advancing again. Or, should we be far from the enemy, we can through unusual energy and activity arrive faster than he expects us.

13. The regular surprise attack (by night as at Hochkirch) is the best way to get the most out of a very small army. But the aggressor, who is

not as well acquainted with the terrain as the defender, is open to many risks. The less well one knows the terrain and the preparations of the enemy, the greater these risks become. In many instances, therefore, these attacks must be considered only as desperate means.

14. This kind of attack demands simpler preparations and a greater concentration of our troops than in the daytime.

3. Principles Governing The Use Of Troops

1. If we cannot dispense with firearms (and if we could, why should we bring them along?), we must use them to open combat. *Cavalry must not be used before the enemy has suffered considerably from our infantry and artillery. From this it follows:*

(a) *That we must place the cavalry behind the infantry. That we must not be easily led to use it in opening combat. Only when the enemy's disorder or his rapid retreat offer the hope of success, should we use our cavalry for an audacious attack.**

2. Artillery fire is much more effective than that of infantry. A battery of eight six-pounders takes up less than one-third of the front taken up

---

* The passages in italics on the following pages are those considered no longer applicable to modern warfare by General Friedrich von Cochenhausen, of the German Academy for Aerial Warfare.

by an infantry battalion; it has less than one-eighth the men of a battalion, and yet its fire is two to three times as effective. On the other hand, artillery has the disadvantage of being less mobile than infantry. This is true, on the whole, even of the lightest horse-artillery, for it cannot, like infantry, be used in any kind of terrain. *It is necessary, therefore, to direct the artillery from the start against the most important points, since it cannot, like infantry, concentrate against these points as the battle progresses. A large battery of 20 to 30 pieces usually decides the battle for that section where it is placed.*

3. From these and other apparent characteristics the following rules can be drawn for the use of the different arms:

(a) We should begin combat with the larger part of our artillery. Only when we have large masses of troops at our disposal should we keep horse and foot-artillery in reserve. *We should use artillery in great batteries massed against one point. Twenty to thirty pieces combined into one battery defend the chief part of our line, or shell that part of the enemy position which we plan to attack.*

(b) After this we use light infantry—either marksmen, riflemen, or fusileers—being careful not to put too many forces into play at the beginning. We try first to discover what lies ahead of us (for we can seldom see that clearly in advance), and which way the battle is turning, etc.

If this firing line is sufficient to counteract the enemy's troops, and if there is no need to hurry, we should do wrong to hasten the use of our remaining forces. We must try to exhaust the enemy as much as possible with this preliminary skirmish.

(c) *If the enemy should lead so many troops into combat that our firing line is about to fall back, or if for some other reason we should no longer hesitate, we must draw up a full line of infantry. This will deploy between 100 and 200 paces from the enemy and will fire or charge, as matters may be.*

(d) *This is the main purpose of the infantry. If, at the same time, the battle-array is deep enough, leaving us another line of infantry (arranged in columns) as reserve, we shall be sufficiently master of the situation at this sector. This second line of infantry should, if possible, be used only in columns to bring about a decision.*

(e) *The cavalry should be as close behind the fighting troops during battle as is possible without great loss; that is, it should be out of the enemy's grape-shot or musket fire.*

On the other hand, it should be close enough to take quick advantage of any favorable turn of battle.

4. In obeying these rules more or less closely, we should never lose sight of the following principle, which I cannot stress enough:

Never bring all our forces into play haphazardly and at one time, thereby losing all means of directing the battle; but fatigue the opponent, if possible, with few forces and conserve a decisive mass for the critical moment. Once this decisive mass has been thrown in, it must be used with the greatest audacity.

5. *We should establish one battle-order (the arrangement of troops before and during combat) for the whole campaign or the whole war. This order will serve in all cases when there is no time for a special disposition of troops. It should, therefore, be calculated primarily for the defensive. This battle-array will introduce a certain uniformity into the fighting-method of the army, which will be useful and advantageous. For it is inevitable that a large part of the lower generals and other officers at the head of small contingents have no special knowledge of tactics and perhaps no outstanding aptitude for the conduct of war.*

Thus there arises a certain methodism in warfare to take the place of art, wherever the latter is absent. In my opinion this is to the highest degree the case in the French armies.

6. *After what I have said about the use of weapons, this battle-order, applied to a brigade, would be approximately as follows:*

:|::|::|::|: Horse Artillery   :|::|::|::|: Horse Artillery

a-b is the line of light infantry, which opens combat and which in rough terrain serves to some extent as an advanced guard. Then comes the artillery, c-d, to be set up at advantageous points. As long as it is not set up, it remains behind the first line of infantry. e-f is the first line of infantry (in this case four battalions) whose purpose is to form into line and to open fire, and g-h are a few regiments of cavalry. i-k is the second line of infantry, which is held in reserve for the decisive stage of the battle, and l-m is its cavalry. A strong corps would be drawn up according to the same principles and in a similar manner. At the same time, it is not essential that the battle-array be exactly like this. It may differ slightly provided that the above principles are followed. So, for instance, in ordinary battle-order the first line of cavalry g-h can remain with the second line of cavalry, l-m. It is to be advanced only in particular cases, when this position should prove to be too far back.

7. The army consists of several such independent corps, which have their own general and staff. They are drawn up in line and behind each other, as described in the general rules for combat. *It should be observed at this point that, unless we are very weak in cavalry, we should create a special cavalry reserve, which, of course, is kept in the rear. Its purpose is as follows:*[10]

(a) *To fall upon the enemy when he is retreating from the field of battle and to attack the cavalry which he uses to cover up his retreat. Should we defeat the enemy's cavalry at this moment, great successes are inevitable, unless the enemy's infantry would perform miracles of bravery. Small detachments of cavalry would not accomplish this purpose.*

(b) *To pursue the enemy more rapidly, if he should be retreating unbeaten or if he should continue to retreat the day after a lost battle.*

Cavalry moves faster than infantry and has a more demoralizing effect on the retreating troops. Next to victory, the act of pursuit is most important in war.

(c) *To execute a great (strategic) turning move, should we need, because of the detour, a branch of the army which moves more rapidly than the infantry.*

In order to make this corps more independent, we should attach a considerable mass of horse-artillery; for a combination of several types of arms can only give greater strength.

8. *The battle-order of troops described thus far was intended for combat; it was the formation of troops for battle.*

The order of march is essentially as follows:

(a) Each independent corps (whether brigade or division) has its own advanced- and rear-guard and forms its own column. That, however, does not prevent several corps from marching one behind the other on the same road, and thus, as it were, forming a single column.

(b) The corps march according to their position in the general formation of battle. They march beside or behind each other, just as they would stand on the battle-field.

(c) *In the corps themselves the following order is invariably observed: the light infantry,*

> *with the addition of one regiment of cav-*
> *alry, forming the advanced and rear-guard,*
> *then the infantry, the artillery, and last the*
> *remaining cavalry.*

This order stands, whether we are moving against
the enemy—in which case it is the natural order—
or parallel with him. In the latter case we should
assume that those troops which in the battle forma-
tion were behind each other should march side by
side. But when we have to draw up the troops
for battle, there will always be sufficient time to
move the cavalry and the second line of infantry
either to the right or left.

4. Principles For The Use Of Terrain

1. The terrain (the ground or country) offers
two advantages in warfare.

The first is that it presents obstacles to the enemy's approach. These either make his advance
impossible at a given point, or force him to march
more slowly and to maintain his formation in columns, etc.

The second advantage is that obstacles in the
terrain enable us to place our troops under cover.

Although both advantages are very important,
I think the second more important than the first.
In any event, it is certain that we profit from it
more frequently, since in most cases even the sim-
plest terrain permits us to place ourselves more

or less under cover. Formerly only the first of
these advantages was known and the second was
rarely used. But today the greater mobility of all
armies has led us to use the former less frequently,
and therefore the latter more frequently. The first
of these two advantages is useful for defense alone,
the second for both offense and defense.

2. The terrain as an obstacle to approach serves
chiefly to support our flank, and to strengthen our
front.

3. To support our flank it must be absolutely
impassable, such as a large river, a lake, an im-
penetrable morass. These obstacles, however, are
very rare, and a complete protection of our flank
is, therefore, hard to find. It is rarer today than
ever before, since we do not stay in one position
very long, but move about a great deal. Consequently we need more positions in the theatre of
war.

An obstacle to approach which is not wholly
impassable is really no *point d'appui* for our flank,
but only a reinforcement. In that case troops must
be drawn up behind it, and for them in turn it
becomes an obstacle to approach.

Yet it is always advantageous to secure our flank
in this way, for then we shall need fewer troops
at this point. But we must beware of two things:
first, of relying so completely on this protection
that we do not keep a strong reserve in the rear;
second, of surrounding ourselves on both flanks

with such obstacles, for, since they do not protect us completely, they do not always prevent fighting on our flanks. They are, therefore, highly detrimental to our defense, for they do not permit us to engage easily in active defense on either wing. We shall be reduced to defense under the most disadvantageous conditions, with both flanks, *a d* and *c b*, thrown back.

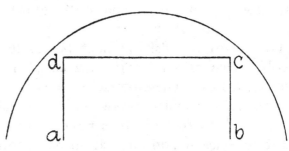

4. The observations just made furnish new arguments for the formation in depth. The less we can find secure support for our flanks, the more corps we must have in the rear to envelop those troops of the enemy which are surrounding us.

5. All kinds of terrain, which cannot be passed by troops marching in line, all villages, all enclosures surrounded by hedges or ditches, marshy meadows, finally all mountains which are crossed only with difficulty, constitute obstacles of this kind. We can pass them, but only slowly and with effort. They increase, therefore, the power of resistance of troops drawn up behind them. Forests are to be included only if they are thickly

wooded and marshy. An ordinary timber-forest
can be passed as easily as a plain. But we must not
overlook the fact that a forest may hide the enemy.
If we conceal ourselves in it, this disadvantage af-
fects both sides. But it is very dangerous, and
thus a grave mistake, to leave forests on our front
or flank unoccupied, unless the forest can be tra-
versed only by a few paths. Barricades built as
obstacles are of little help, since they can easily
be removed.

6. From all this it follows that we should use
such obstacles on one flank to put up a relatively
strong resistance with few troops, while executing
our planned offensive on the other flank. It is
very advantageous to combine the use of entrenchments with such natural obstacles, because then,
if the enemy should pass the obstacle, the fire from
these entrenchments will protect our weak troops
against too great superiority and sudden rout.

7. When we are defending ourselves, any obstacle on our front is of great value.

Mountains are occupied only for this reason.
For an elevated position seldom has any important
influence, often none at all, on the effectiveness
of arms. But if we stand on a height, the enemy,
in order to approach us, must climb laboriously.
He will advance but slowly, become separated, and
arrive with his forces exhausted. Given equal bravery and strength, these advantages may be decisive. On no account should we overlook the

moral effect of a rapid, running assault. It hardens
the advancing soldier against danger, while the
stationary soldier loses his presence of mind. *It is,
therefore, always very advantageous to put our first
line of infantry and artillery upon a mountain.*

Often the grade of the mountain is so steep, or
its slope so undulating and uneven, that it cannot
be effectively swept by gun-fire. In that case we
should not place our first line, but at the most
only our sharp-shooters, at the edge of the mountain. Our full line we should place in such a way
that the enemy is subject to its most effective fire
the moment he reaches the top and reassembles
his forces.

All other obstacles to approach, such as small
rivers, brooks, ravines, etc., serve to break the
enemy's front. He will have to re-form his lines
after passing them and thus will be delayed. These
obstacles must, therefore, be placed under our
most effective fire, *which is grape-shot (400 to
600 paces), if we have a great deal of artillery or
musket-shot (150 to 200 paces), if we have little
artillery at this point.*

8. It is, therefore, a basic law to place all obstacles to approach, which are to strengthen our
front, under our most effective fire. But it is important to notice that we must never completely
limit our resistance to this fire *but must hold ready
for a bayonet-charge an important part of our
troops (1/3 to 1/2) organized into columns. Should*

*we be very weak, therefore, we must place only
our firing-line, composed of riflemen and artillery,
close enough to keep the obstacle under fire. The
rest of our troops, organized into columns, we
should keep 600 to 800 paces back, if possible under cover.*

9. Another method of using these obstacles to
protect our front is to leave them a short distance
ahead. They are thus within the effective range
of our cannon (*1000 to 2000 paces*) and we can
attack the enemy's columns from all sides, as they
emerge. (Something like this was done by Duke
Ferdinand at Minden.[4] In this way the obstacle
contributes to our plan of active defense, and this
active defense, of which we spoke earlier, will be
executed on our front.

10. Thus far we have considered the obstacles
of the ground and country primarily as connected
lines related to extended positions. It is still necessary to say something about isolated points.

On the whole we can defend single, isolated
points only by entrenchments or strong obstacles
of terrain. We shall not discuss the first here. The
only obstacles of terrain which can be held by
themselves are:

(a) Isolated, steep heights.

Here entrenchments are likewise indispensable; for the enemy can always move
against the defender with a more or less
extended front. And the latter will always

end up by being taken from the rear, since one is rarely strong enough to make front towards all sides.

(b) Defiles.

By this term we mean any narrow path, through which the enemy can advance only against one point. Bridges, dams, and steep ravines belong here.

We should observe that these obstacles fall into two categories: either the aggressor can in no way avoid them, as for example bridges across large rivers, in which case the defender can boldly draw up his whole force so as to fire upon the point of crossing as effectively as possible. Or we are not absolutely sure that the enemy can not turn the obstacle, as with bridges across small streams and most mountain defiles. In that case it is necessary to reserve a considerable part of our troops 1/3 to 1/2 for an attack in close order.

(c) Localities, villages, small towns, etc.

With very brave troops, who fight enthusiastically, houses offer a unique defense for few against many. But, if we are not sure of the individual soldier, it is preferable to occupy the houses, gardens, etc., only with sharp-shooters and the entrances to the village with cannons. The greater part of our troops *(1/2 to 3/4) we should keep in*

close columns and hidden in the locality or
behind it, so as to fall upon the enemy while
he is invading.

11. These isolated posts serve in large operations
partly as outposts, in which case they serve not as
absolute defense but only as a delay to the enemy,
and partly to hold points which are important for
the combinations we have planned for our army.
Also it is often necessary to hold on to a remote
point in order to gain time for the development
of active measures of defense which we may have
planned. But, if a point is remote, it is *ipso facto*
isolated.

12. Two more observations about isolated obstacles are necessary. The first is that we must keep
troops ready behind them to receive detachments
that have been thrown back. The second is that
whoever includes such isolated obstacles in his defensive combinations should never count on them
too much, no matter how strong the obstacle may
be. On the other hand, the military leader to
whom the defense of the obstacle has been entrusted must always try to hold out, even under
the most adverse circumstances. For this there is
needed a spirit of determination and self-sacrifice,
which finds its source only in ambition and enthu-
siasm. We must, therefore, choose men for this
mission who are not lacking in these noble qualities.

13. Using terrain to cover the disposition and
advance of troops needs no detailed exposition.

We should not occupy the crest of the mountain which we intend to defend (as has been done so frequently in the past) but draw up behind it. We should not take our position in front of a forest, but inside or behind it; the latter only if we are able to survey the forest or thicket. *We should keep our troops in columns, so as to find cover more easily.* We must make use of villages, small thickets, and rolling terrain to hide our troops. For our advance we should choose the most intersected country, etc.

In cultivated country, which can be reconnoitered so easily, there is almost no region that can not hide a large part of the defender's troops if they have made clever use of obstacles. To cover the aggressor's advance is more difficult, since he must follow the roads.

It goes without saying that in using the terrain to hide our troops, we must never lose sight of the goal and combinations we have set for ourselves. Above all things we should not break up our battle-order completely, even though we may deviate slightly from it.

14. If we recapitulate what has been said about terrain, the following appears most important for the defender, *i.e.*, for the choice of positions:

(a) Support of one or both flanks.

(b) Open view on front and flanks.

(c) Obstacles to approach on the front.

(d) Masked disposition of troops. And finally

(e) Intersected country in the rear, to render pursuit more difficult in case of defeat. But no defiles too near (as at Friedland), since they cause delay and confusion.[11]

15. It would be pedantic to believe that all these advantages could be found in any position we may take up during a war. Not all positions are of equal importance: the most important are those in which we most likely may be attacked. It is here that we should try to have all these advantages, while in others we only need part.

16. The two main points which the aggressor should consider in regard to the choice of terrain are not to select too difficult a terrain for the attack, but on the other hand to advance, if possible, through a terrain in which the enemy can least survey our force.

17. I close these observations with a principle which is of highest significance, and which must be considered the keystone of the whole defensive theory:

NEVER TO DEPEND COMPLETELY ON THE STRENGTH OF THE TERRAIN AND CONSEQUENTLY NEVER TO BE ENTICED INTO PASSIVE DEFENSE BY A STRONG TERRAIN.

For if the terrain is really so strong that the aggressor cannot possibly expel us, he will turn it, which is always possible, and thus render the strongest terrain useless. We shall be forced into battle under very different circumstances, and in a completely different terrain, and we might as well not have included the first terrain in our plans. But if the terrain is not so strong, and if an attack within its confines is still possible, its advantages can never make up for the disadvantages of passive defense. All obstacles are useful, therefore, only for partial defense, in order that we may put up a relatively strong resistance with few troops and gain time for the offensive, through which we try to win a real victory elsewhere.

III. STRATEGY

This term means the combination of individual engagements to attain the goal of the campaign or war.

If we know how to fight and how to win, little more knowledge is needed. For it is easy to combine fortunate results. It is merely a matter of experienced judgment and does not depend on special knowledge, as does the direction of battle.

The few principles, therefore, which come up in this connection, and which depend primarily on the condition of the respective states and armies, can in their essential parts be very briefly summarized:

1. General Principles

1. Warfare has three main objects:
   (a) To conquer and destroy the armed power of the enemy;
   (b) To take possession of his material and other sources of strength, and
   (c) To gain public opinion.

2. To accomplish the first purpose, we should always direct our principal operation against the main body of the enemy army or at least against an important portion of his forces. For only after defeating these can we pursue the other two objects successfully.

3. In order to seize the enemy's material forces we should direct our operations against the places

where most of these resources are concentrated: principal cities, storehouses, and large fortresses. On the way to these objectives we shall encounter the enemy's main force or at least a considerable part of it.

4. Public opinion is won through great victories and the occupation of the enemy's capital.

5. The first and most important rule to observe in order to accomplish these purposes, is to use our entire forces with the utmost energy. Any moderation shown would leave us short of our aim. Even with everything in our favor, we should be unwise not to make the greatest effort in order to make the result perfectly certain. For such effort can never produce negative results. Suppose the country suffers greatly from this, no lasting disadvantage will arise; for the greater the effort, the sooner the suffering will cease.

The moral impression created by these actions is of infinite importance. They make everyone confident of success, which is the best means for suddenly raising the nation's morale.

6. The second rule is to concentrate our power as much as possible against that section where the chief blows are to be delivered and to incur disadvantages elsewhere, so that our chances of success may increase at the decisive point. This will compensate for all other disadvantages.

7. The third rule is never to waste time. Unless important advantages are to be gained from hesita-

tion, it is necessary to set to work at once. By this speed a hundred enemy measures are nipped in the bud, and public opinion is won most rapidly.

Surprise plays a much greater role in strategy than in tactics. It is the most important element of victory. Napoleon, Frederick II, Gustavus Adolphus, Cæsar, Hannibal, and Alexander owe the brightest rays of their fame to their swiftness.

8. Finally, the fourth rule is to follow up our successes with the utmost energy.

Only pursuit of the beaten enemy gives the fruits of victory.

9. The first of these rules serves as a basis for the other three. If we have observed it, we can be as daring as possible with the last three, and yet not risk our all. For it provides us with the means of constantly creating new forces in our rear, and with fresh forces any misfortune can be remedied.

Therein lies the caution which deserves to be called wise, and not in taking each step forward with timidity.

10. Small states cannot wage wars of conquest in our times. But in defensive warfare even the means of small states are infinitely great. I am, therefore, firmly convinced that if we spare no effort to reappear again and again with new masses of troops, if we use all possible means of preparation and keep our forces concentrated at the main point, and if we, thus prepared, pursue a great

aim with determination and energy, we have done all that can be done on a large scale for the strategic direction of the war. And unless we are very unfortunate in battle we are bound to be victorious to the same extent that our opponent lags behind in effort and energy.

11. In observing these principles little depends on the form in which the operations are carried out. I shall try, nevertheless, to make clear in a few words the most important aspects of this question.

In tactics we always seek to envelop that part of the enemy against which we direct our main attack. We do this partly because our forces are more effective in a concentric than in a parallel attack, and further because we can only thus cut off the enemy from his line of retreat.

But if we apply this to the whole theatre of war (and consequently to the enemy's lines of communication), the individual columns and armies, which are to envelop the enemy, are in most cases too far away from each other to participate in one and the same engagement. The opponent will find himself in the middle and will be able to turn against the corps one by one and defeat them all with a single army. Frederick II's campaigns may serve as examples, especially those of 1757 and 1758.[12]

The individual engagement, therefore, remains the principal decisive event. Consequently, if we

attack concentrically without having decisive superiority, we shall lose in battle all the advantages,
which we expected from our enveloping attack
on the enemy. For an attack on the lines of communication takes effect only very slowly, while victory on the field of battle bears fruit immediately.

In strategy, therefore, the side that is surrounded
by the enemy is better off than the side which sur-
rounds its opponent, especially with equal or even
weaker forces.

Colonel Jomini was right in this, and if Mr. von
Bülow has demonstrated the opposite with so
much semblance of truth, it is only because he
attributed too great an importance to the inter-
ruption of provisions and carelessly and completely denied the inevitable success of battle.[13]

To cut the enemy's line of retreat, however, strategic envelopment or a turning movement is very
effective. But we can achieve this, if necessary,
through tactical envelopment. A strategic move is,
therefore, advisable only if we are so superior
(physically and morally) that we shall be strong
enough at the principal point to dispense with the
detached corps.

The Emperor Napoleon never engaged in strategic envelopment, although he was often, indeed
almost always, both physically and morally superior.[14]

Frederick II used it only once, in 1757, in his
invasion of Bohemia.[15] To be sure, the result was

that the Austrians could not give battle until
Prague, and what good was the conquest of Bohemia as far as Prague without a decisive victory?
The battle of Kolin forced him to give up all this
territory again, which proves that battles decide
everything. At the same time he was obviously in
danger at Prague of being attacked by the whole
Austrian force, before Schwerin arrived. He would
not have run this risk had he passed through Saxony
with all his forces. In that case, the first battle
would have been fought perhaps near Budin, on
the Eger, and it would have been as decisive as
that of Prague. The dislocation of the Prussian
army during the winter in Silesia and Saxony un-
doubtedly caused this concentric maneuver. It is
important to notice that circumstances of this kind
are generally more influential than the advantages
to be gained by the form of attack. For facility
of operations increases their speed, and the friction
inherent in the tremendous war-machine of an
armed power is so great in itself that it should not
be increased unnecessarily.

12. Moreover, the principle of concentrating
our forces as much as possible on the main point
diverts us from the idea of strategic envelopment
and the deployment of our forces follows auto-
matically. I was right, therefore, in saying that the
form of this deployment is of little consequence.
There is, however, one case in which a strategic
move against the enemy's flank will lead to great

successes similar to those of a battle: if in a poor
country the enemy has accumulated with great effort stores of supplies, on whose preservation his
operations absolutely depend. In this case it may
be advisable not to march our main forces against
those of the enemy, but to attack his base of supply.
For this, however, two conditions are essential:

(a) The enemy must be so far from his base that
our threat will force him into a considerable
retreat, and

(b) We must be able to obstruct his advance in
the direction followed by his principal
force with only a few troops (thanks to
natural and artificial obstacles), so that he
cannot make conquests somewhere else
which will compensate for the loss of his
base.

13. The provisioning of troops is a necessary
condition of warfare and thus has great influence
on the operations, especially since it permits only
a limited concentration of troops and since it helps
to determine the theatre of war through the choice
of a line of operations.

14. The provisioning of troops is carried on, if
a region possibly permits it, through requisitions at
the expense of the region.

In the modern method of war armies take up
considerably more territory than before. The crea-
tion of distinct, independent corps has made this
possible, without putting ourselves at a disadvan-

tage before an adversary who follows the old method of concentration at a single point (with from 70,000 to 100,000 men). For an independent corps, organized as they now are, can withstand for some time an enemy two or three times its superior. Then the others will arrive and, even if the first corps has already been beaten, it has not fought in vain, as we have had occasion to remark.

Today, therefore, the divisions and corps move into battle independently, marching side by side or behind each other and only close enough to take part in the same battle, if they belong to the same army.

This makes possible immediate provisioning without storehouses. The very organization of the corps with their General Staff and their Commissariat facilitates this.

15. If there are no MORE decisive motives (as for example the location of the enemy's main army), we choose the most fertile provinces for our operations; for facility of provisioning increases the speed of our actions. Only the situation of the enemy's main force which we are seeking out, only the location of his capital and the place of arms which we wish to conquer are more important than provisioning. All other considerations, such as the advantageous disposition of our forces, of which we have already spoken, are as a rule much less important.

16. In spite of these new methods of provision-

ing, it is quite impossible to do without any depots whatever. Therefore, even when the resources of the region are quite sufficient, a wise military leader does not fail to establish depots in his rear for unexpected emergencies and in order to be able to concentrate his forces at certain points. This precaution is of the sort which are not taken at the expense of the final goal.

2. Defensive

1. Politically speaking defensive war is a war which we wage for our independence. Strategically it is the kind of campaign in which we limit ourselves to fighting the enemy in a theatre of war which we have prepared for this purpose. Whether the battles which we wage in this theatre of war are offensive or defensive, makes no difference.

2. We adopt a strategic defensive mainly when the enemy is superior. Fortresses and intrenched camps, which constitute the chief preparations for a theatre of war, afford, of course, great advantages, to which may be added the knowledge of the terrain and the possession of good maps. A smaller army, or an army which is based on a smaller state and more limited resources, will be better able to withstand the enemy WITH these advantages than without them.

In addition there are the following two reasons which can lead us to choose a defensive war.

First, when the regions surrounding the theatre

of war render operations extremely difficult because of lack of provisions. In this case we avoid
a disadvantage which the enemy is forced to un-
dergo. This is the case now (1812) with the Russian army.

Second, when the enemy is superior in warfare.
In a theatre of war which we have prepared, which
we know, and in which all minor conditions are in
our favor, war is easier to conduct, and we com-
mit fewer mistakes. When lack of trust in our
troops and generals forces us to wage defensive
war, we often like to combine tactical with strategic defensive. In that case we fight battles in
prepared positions because we are thus again ex-
posed to fewer mistakes.

3. In defensive just as in offensive warfare, it is
necessary to pursue a great aim: the destruction of
the enemy army, either by battle or by rendering
its subsistence extremely difficult. Thus we shall
disorganize it and force it into a retreat, during
which it will necessarily suffer great losses. Wellington's campaign in 1810 and 1811 is a good
example.[16]

Defensive warfare, therefore, does not consist
of waiting idly for things to happen. We must
wait only if it brings us visible and decisive advantages. That calm before the storm, when the aggressor is gathering new forces for a great blow,
is most dangerous for the defender.

If the Austrians after the battle of Aspern had

increased their forces threefold, as they might have and as the Emperor Napoleon did, then and only then would they have made good use of the lull which lasted until the battle of Wagram. This they did not do, and consequently the time was lost. It would have been wiser to profit from Napoleon's disadvantageous position, and to gather the fruits of the battle of Aspern.[17]

4. The purpose of fortifications is to keep a considerable part of the enemy's army occupied as siege troops, to give us an opportunity to defeat the rest of his army. Consequently, it is best to fight our battles behind our fortifications and not in front of them. But we must not stand by idly, while they are being conquered, as Bennigsen did during the siege of Danzig.[18]

5. Large rivers, across which it is difficult to throw a bridge (such as the Danube below Vienna and the Lower Rhine), offer a natural line of defense. But we should not distribute our forces evenly along the river bank in order to prevent any crossing whatsoever. That would be most dangerous. On the contrary, we should watch the river and fall upon the enemy from all sides the minute he crosses, while he has not yet reassembled his forces and is still restricted to a narrow space on the river bank. The battle of Aspern offers a good illustration. At Wagram the Austrians had yielded to the French too much territory without the slightest necessity, so that the

disadvantages inherent in a river crossing had disappeared.[19]

6. Mountains are the second obstacle which offers a good line of defense. There are two ways of using them. The first is to leave them in front of us, occupying them only with light troops and considering them, so to speak, a river which the enemy will have to cross. As soon as his separated columns emerge from the passes, we fall upon one of them with all our force. The second is to occupy the mountains ourselves. In that case we must defend each pass with just a small corps and keep an important part of the army (1/3-1/2) in reserve, in order to attack with superior forces one of the enemy columns that succeed in breaking through. We must not divide up this large reserve to prevent completely the penetration of any enemy columns, but must plan from the outset to fall only upon those columns which we suppose to be the strongest. If we thus defeat an important part of the attacking army, any other columns which have succeeded in breaking through will withdraw of their own accord.

In the midst of most mountain formations we find more or less elevated plains (plateaus) whose slopes are cut by ravines serving as means of access. Mountains, therefore, offer the defender a region in which he can move rapidly to the right or left, while the columns of the aggressor remain separated by steep, inaccessible ridges. Only mountains of this kind are well adapted for defensive warfare. If, on the other hand, their whole interior is rough and inaccessible, leaving the defender dispersed and divided, their defense by the bulk of the army is a dangerous undertaking. For under these circumstances all advantages are on the side of the aggressor, who can attack certain points with great superiority, and no pass, no isolated point is so strong that it cannot be taken within a day by superior forces.

7. In regard to mountain warfare in general, we should observe that everything depends on the skill of our subordinate officers and still more on the morale of our soldiers. Here it is not a question of skillful maneuvering, but of warlike spirit and whole-hearted devotion to the cause; for each man is left more or less to act independently. That is why national militias are especially suited for mountain warfare. While they lack the ability to maneuver, they possess the other qualities to the highest degree.

8. Finally, it should be observed that strategic defensive, though it is stronger than the offensive, should serve only to win the first important successes. If these are won and peace does not follow immediately, we can gain further successes only through the offensive. For if we remain continually on the defensive, we run the great risk of always waging war at our own expense. This no state can endure indefinitely. If it submits to the

blows of its adversary without ever striking back, it will very likely become exhausted and succumb. We must begin, therefore, using the defensive, so as to end more successfully by the offensive.

3. Offensive

1. The strategic offensive pursues the aim of the war directly, aiming straight at the destruction of the enemy's forces, while the strategic defensive seeks to reach this purpose indirectly. The principles of the offensive are therefore already contained in the "General Principles" of strategy. Only two points need be mentioned more fully.

2. The first is constant replacement of troops and arms. This is easier for the defender, because of the proximity of his sources of supply. The aggressor, although he controls in most cases a larger state, must usually gather his forces from a distance and therefore with great difficulty. Lest he find himself short of effectives, he must organize the recruiting of troops and the transport of arms a long time before they are needed. The roads of our lines of operation must be covered constantly with transports of soldiers and supplies. We must establish military stations along these roads to hasten this rapid transport.

3. Even under the most favorable circumstances and with greatest moral and physical superiority, the aggressor should foresee a possibility of great disaster. He therefore must organize on his lines

of operation strong points to which he can retreat with a defeated army. Such are fortresses with fortified camps or simply fortified camps.

Large rivers offer the best means of halting the pursuing enemy for a while. We must therefore secure our crossing by means of bridgeheads, surrounded by a number of strong redoubts.

We must leave behind us a number of troops for the occupation of these strong points as well as the occupation of the most important cities and fortresses. Their number depends on how much we have to be afraid of invasions or of the attitude of the inhabitants. These troops, together with reinforcements, form new corps, which, in case of success, follow the advancing army, but in case of misfortune, occupy the fortified points in order to secure our retreat.

Napoleon always took great care with these measures for the protection of the rear of his army, and therefore, in his most audacious operations, risked less than was usually apparent.

IV. APPLICATION OF THESE PRINCIPLES IN TIME OF WAR

The principles of the art of war are in themselves extremely simple and quite within the reach of sound common sense. Even though they require more special knowledge in tactics than in strategy, this knowledge is of such small scope, that it does not compare with any other subject in extent and variety. Extensive knowledge and deep learning are by no means necessary, nor are extraordinary intellectual faculties. If, in addition to experienced judgment, a special mental quality is required, it would be, after all that has been said, cunning or shrewdness. For a long time the contrary has been maintained, either because of false veneration for the subject or because of the vanity of the authors who have written about it. Unprejudiced reflection should convince us of this, and experience only makes this conviction stronger. As recently as the Revolutionary War we find many men who proved themselves able military leaders, yes, even military leaders of the first order, without having had any military education. In the case of Condé, Wallenstein, Suvorov, and a multitude of others[20] it is very doubtful whether or not they had the advantage of such education.

The conduct of war itself is without doubt very difficult. But the difficulty is not that erudition and great genius are necessary to understand the basic principles of warfare. These principles are within the reach of any well-organized mind, which is unprejudiced and not entirely unfamiliar with the subject. Even the application of these principles on maps or on paper presents no difficulty, and to have devised a good plan of operations is no great masterpiece. The great difficulty is this:

TO REMAIN FAITHFUL THROUGHOUT
TO THE PRINCIPLES WE HAVE LAID
DOWN FOR OURSELVES.

To call attention to this difficulty is the purpose of these closing remarks, and to give Your Royal Highness a clear idea of it I consider the most important object of this essay.

The conduct of war resembles the workings of an intricate machine with tremendous friction, so that combinations which are easily planned on paper can be executed only with great effort.

The free will and the mind of the military commander, therefore, find themselves constantly hampered, and one needs a remarkable strength of mind and soul to overcome this resistance. Many good ideas have perished because of this friction, and we must carry out more simply and moderately what under a more complicated form would have given greater results.

It may be impossible to enumerate exhaustively the causes of this friction; but the main ones are as follows:

1. Generally we are not nearly as well acquainted with the position and measures of the enemy as we assume in our plan of operations. The minute we begin carrying out our decision, a thousand doubts arise about the dangers which might develop if we have been seriously mistaken in our plan. A feeling of uneasiness, which often takes hold of a person about to perform something great, will take possession of us, and from this uneasiness to indecision, and from there to half measures are small, scarcely discernible steps.

2. Not only are we uncertain about the strength of the enemy, but in addition rumor (*i.e.*, all the news which we obtain from outposts, through spies, or by accident) exaggerates his size. The majority of people are timid by nature, and that is why they constantly exaggerate danger. All influences on the military leader, therefore, combine to give him a false impression of his opponent's strength, and from this arises a new source of indecision.

We cannot take this uncertainty too seriously, and it is important to be prepared for it from the beginning.

After we have thought out everything carefully in advance and have sought and found without prejudice the most plausible plan, we must not be ready to abandon it at the slightest provocation. On the contrary, we must be prepared to submit the reports which reach us to careful criticism, we must compare them with each other, and send out for more. In this way false reports are very often disproved immediately, and the first reports confirmed. In both cases we gain certainty and can make our decision accordingly. Should this certainty be lacking, we must tell ourselves that nothing is accomplished in warfare without daring; that the nature of war certainly does not let us see at all times where we are going; that what is probable will always be probable though at the moment it may not seem so; and finally, that we cannot be readily ruined by a single error, if we have made reasonable preparations.

3. Our uncertainty about the situation at a given moment is not limited to the conditions of the enemy only but of our own army as well. The latter can rarely be kept together to the extent that we are able to survey all its parts at any moment, and if we are inclined to uneasiness, new doubts will arise. We shall want to wait, and a delay of our whole plan will be the inevitable result.

We must, therefore, be confident that the general measures we have adopted will produce the results we expect. Most important in this connection is the trust which we must have in our lieutenants. Consequently, it is important to choose men on whom we can rely and to put aside all other considerations. If we have made appropriate preparations, taking into account all possible misfortunes, so that we shall not be lost immediately if they occur, we must boldly advance into the shadows of uncertainty.

4. If we wage war with all our strength, our subordinate commanders and even our troops (especially if they are not used to warfare) will frequently encounter difficulties which they declare insurmountable. They find the march too long, the fatigue too great, the provisions impossible. If we lend our ear to all these DIFFICULTIES, as Frederick II called them, we shall soon succumb completely, and instead of acting with force and determination, we shall be reduced to weakness and inactivity.

To resist all this we must have faith in our own insight and convictions. At the time this often has the appearance of stubbornness, but in reality it is that strength of mind and character which is called firmness.

5. The results on which we count in warfare are never as precise as is imagined by someone who has not carefully observed a war and become used to it.

Very often we miscalculate the march of a column by several hours, without being able to tell the cause of the delay. Often we encounter obstacles which were impossible to foresee. Often we intend to reach a certain place with our army and fall short of it by several hours. Often a small outpost which we have set up achieves much less than we expected, while an enemy outpost achieves much more. Often the resources of a region do not amount to as much as we expected, etc.

We can triumph over such obstacles only with very great exertion, and to accomplish this the leader must show a severity bordering on cruelty. Only when he knows that everything possible is always being done, can he be sure that these small difficulties will not have a great influence on his operations. Only then can he be sure that he will not fall too far short of the aim which he could have reached.

6. We may be sure that an army will never be in the condition supposed by someone following its operations from an armchair. If he is sympathetic to the army he will imagine it from a third to a half stronger and better than it really is. It is quite natural that the military commander will make the same mistake in planning his first operations. Consequently, he will see his army melt away as he never thought it would, and his cavalry and artillery become useless. What appeared possible and easy to the observer and to the commander at the opening of a campaign is often difficult and even impossible to carry out. If the military leader is filled with high ambition and if he pursues his aims with audacity and strength of will, he will reach them in spite of all obstacles; while an ordinary person would have found in the condition of his army a sufficient excuse for giving in.

Masséna proved at Genoa and in Portugal the influence of a strong-willed leader over his troops. At Genoa, the limitless exertion to which his strength of will, not to say his harshness, forced people, was crowned with success. In Portugal he at least retreated later than anyone else would have.[21]

Most of the time the enemy army is in the same position. For example, Wallenstein and Gustavus Adolphus at Nuremberg,[22] and Napoleon and Bennigsen after the battle of Eylau.[23] But while we do not see the condition of the enemy, our own is right before our eyes. The latter, therefore, makes a greater impression on ordinary people than the first, since sensuous impressions are stronger for such people than the language of reason.

7. The provisioning of troops, no matter how it is done, whether through storehouses or requisitions, always presents such difficulty that it must have a decisive influence on the choice of operations. It is often contrary to the most effective combination, and forces us to search for provisions when we would like to pursue victory and brilliant success. This is the main cause for the unwieldiness of the whole war machine which keeps the results so far beneath the flight of our great plans.

A general, who with tyrannical authority demands of his troops the most extreme exertions and the greatest privations, and an army which in the course of long wars has become hardened to such sacrifices will have a tremendous advantage over their adversaries and will reach their aim much faster in spite of all obstacles. With equally good plans, what a difference of result!

8. We cannot stress the following too much:

Visual impressions gained during actual combat are more vivid than those gained beforehand by mature reflection. But they give us only the outward appearance of things, which, as we know, rarely corresponds to their essence. We therefore run the risk of sacrificing mature reflection for first impression.

The natural timidity of humans, which sees only one side to everything, makes this first impression incline toward fear and exaggerated caution.

Therefore we must fortify ourselves against this impression and have blind faith in the results of our own earlier reflections, in order to strengthen ourselves against the weakening impressions of the moment.

These difficulties, therefore, demand confidence and firmness of conviction. That is why the study of military history is so important, for it makes us see things as they are and as they function. The principles which we can learn from theoretical instruction are only suited to facilitate this study and to call our attention to the most important elements in the history of war.

Your Royal Highness, therefore, must become acquainted with these principles in order to check them against the history of war, to see whether they are in agreement with it and to discover where they are corrected or even contradicted by the course of events.

In addition, only the study of military history is capable of giving those who have no experience of their own a clear impression of what I have just called the friction of the whole machine.

Of course, we must not be satisfied with its main conclusions, and still less with the reasoning of historians, but we must penetrate as deeply as possible into the details. For the aim of historians rarely is to present the absolute truth. Usually they wish to embellish the deeds of their army or to demonstrate the concordance of events with their imaginary rules. They invent history instead of writing it. We need not study much history for the purpose we propose. The detailed knowledge of a few individual engagements is more useful than the general knowledge of a great many campaigns. It is therefore more useful to read detailed accounts and diaries than regular works of history. An example of such an account, which cannot be surpassed, is the description of the defense of Menin in 1794, in the memoirs of General von Scharnhorst. This narrative, especially the part which tells of the sortie and break through the enemy lines, gives Your Royal

Highness an example of how to write military history.[24]

No battle in history has convinced me as much as this one that we must not despair of success in war until the last moment. It proves that the influence of good principles, which never manifests itself as often as we expect, can suddenly reappear, even under the most unfortunate circumstances, and when we have already given up hope of their influence.

A powerful emotion must stimulate the great ability of a military leader, whether it be ambition as in Caesar, hatred of the enemy as in Hannibal, or the pride in a glorious defeat, as in Frederick the Great.

Open your heart to such emotion. Be audacious and cunning in your plans, firm and persevering in their execution, determined to find a glorious end, and fate will crown your youthful brow with a shining glory, which is the ornament of princes, and engrave your image in the hearts of your last descendants.

NOTES

1. FREDERICK II ("the Great"), King of Prussia from 1740-1786, is one of the great military figures of history. The first half of his reign was largely devoted to war, with Austria under Maria Theresa as his chief adversary and Silesia as a major cause: the first and second SILESIAN WARS (1740-45) and the Seven Years' War (1756-63).

It was especially during the latter war, when Prussia, allied with England, had to fight the superior alliance of Austria, France, Russia, Sweden, and Saxony, that Frederick proved his unusual skill and audacity as a military leader. One of his most brilliant and decisive victories was won near the Silesian village of LEUTHEN (Dec. 5, 1757). This victory against a vastly superior Austrian army under Prince Charles of Lorraine was due to Frederick's military genius as well as the excellent morale of his officers and men. Before the battle, in the presence of his generals, the King delivered a famous address, which illustrates Clausewitz' point. It ended thus: "Gentlemen, the enemy stands behind his entrenchments, armed to the teeth. We must attack him and win, or else perish. Nobody must think of getting through any other way. If you do not like this you may hand in your resignation and go home."

(Other significant battles of the Seven Years' War, mentioned by Clausewitz, were the battles

of Rossbach, Liegnitz, Prague, Kolin, Hochkirch,
and Minden.)

2. The term "corps" as used throughout by
Clausewitz does not refer to a specific army unit
(such as a modern army-corps) but is used simply
to describe any section of the army.

3. Both battles were part of Napoleon's campaign against Austria in 1809. At Eckmühl, near
RATISBON, in Southern Germany, a French army
under Napoleon and his Marshal Davout defeated
a strong Austrian army on April 22. This paved
the way for Napoleon's invasion of Austria, where
at the village of WAGRAM, near Vienna, he succeeded in beating the Archduke Charles so thoroughly (July 5-6) that Austria had to ask for an
armistice shortly afterwards.

(For further references to these battles see pages
20, 23, 55.)

4. Near MINDEN in Westphalia, DUKE FERDINAND
OF BRUNSWICK, one of Frederick II's generals during the Seven Years' War, won a significant victory over the French under Marshal Contades.
He had planned to attack the French positions in
the early hours of August 1, 1759, when he received word that the French in turn were getting
ready to attack him. He went through with his
plans for mobilization, thus completely upsetting
Contades' preparations for a surprise attack. In
the ensuing battle the allied Prussian, English and
Hanoverian troops won a decisive victory, which

resulted in the withdrawal of the French beyond the Rhine and Main rivers.

At the same time, about one-third of Ferdinand's army, organized as an independent corps under General von Wangenheim, was stationed to the left of the main army, near the village of TANNHAUSEN (also known as Thonhausen, or Thodthausen). This corps had not been informed of the impending attack of the French. An enemy corps under Broglie opened fire on Wangenheim's entrenchments around 5 A.M. It failed to follow up its surprise attack, however, thus enabling Wangenheim to draw up his troops and resist Broglie until the defeat of the main army under Contades forced the French to retreat.

5. At ROSSBACH, on November 5, 1757, FREDERICK II's army of 22,000 men defeated a combined French and German army twice its size, under the leadership of the incompetent Princes of Soubise (France) and Hildburghausen (Saxony). While his opponents, thinking he was beating a hasty retreat, began their pursuit, Frederick's excellently trained cavalry under General von Seydlitz suddenly attacked their right flank. The enemy, with no time to draw up in battle-formation, was completely dispersed and defeated.

The moral effect of Frederick's victory inside and outside of Germany was tremendous. It reestablished his reputation, which had suffered considerably after his defeat at Kolin (see note 15).

6. The Battle of LIEGNITZ, like those of Rossbach and Leuthen earlier, shows FREDERICK the Great's skill in defeating a superior force by using his highly mobile army in a concentrated attack, keeping the enemy as much in the dark about his intentions as possible.

Finding himself surrounded near Liegnitz (Saxony) by several Austrian armies numbering close to 100,000, he planned a careful withdrawal. During the night of August 14-15, 1760, he broke camp, leaving his fires burning, however, to deceive the enemy, who had planned a three-cornered attack for the morning of August 15. At dawn the Prussian King surprised one section of the Austrian army under Laudon on the river Katzbach, and defeated 30,000 men with an army half this size.

7. During Napoleon's campaign against the Second Coalition (Great Britain, Austria, and Russia), the French General MOREAU had concentrated his forces at the village of HOHENLINDEN, situated in the midst of a great forest on a plateau east of Munich. Despite the warnings of his generals, Archduke John of Austria entered the forest on Dec. 2, 1800, to seek the French. Meanwhile Moreau, hidden by the forest, moved part of his forces, outflanked the Austrians, and caught them between two fires. The Austrian army was thoroughly beaten, losing more than 20,000 men, and Moreau was free to continue his advance toward Vienna.

8. FREDERICK II achieved the necessary concentration of his forces by a peculiar battle-order known as "schiefe Schlachtordnung" (oblique formation). Though by no means new (it had been used occasionally since antiquity), it was Frederick who first applied this formation consistently in almost all his battles. In his *General Principles of Warfare*, written in 1748, Frederick described it as follows: "We 'refuse' one of our wings to the enemy and strengthen the wing with which we plan to attack." This would make possible the defeat of a vastly superior enemy: "An army of 100,000 men, thus attacked on its flank, can be beaten by 30,000 men." The most successful example of Frederick's use of this formation "in echelon" was the battle of Leuthen (see note 1).

9. At HOCHKIRCH, a village in Saxony, the Austrian army of Marshal Daun delivered a serious defeat to Frederick II's forces on October 14, 1758. Attacking at the crack of dawn, the Austrians caught the over-confident King of Prussia unprepared, and with a force of 78,000 they defeated his army of 40,000, inflicting heavy losses on the Prussians. About 9,000 men were lost and several of Frederick's generals were killed or wounded.

10. General Friedrich von Cochenhausen in his edition of this book points out that most of the rules dealing with this cavalry reserve, though no longer valid in modern warfare, can be applied almost word for word to mechanized units.

11. At FRIEDLAND, in East Prussia, a Russian army under Bennigsen was defeated by Napoleon, on June 14, 1807, during the war of the Third Coalition against France. The Russians were withdrawing along the right bank of the river Alle, towards Koenigsberg, when they met a single French corps under the command of Marshal Lannes. Bennigsen thought this an excellent chance for an attack, but Lannes held out until Napoleon arrived with his main army. The Emperor concentrated his attack on the Russian left wing, which was separated from the right wing by a ravine, and whose only possible retreat was through a narrow outlet between this ravine and the river. Napoleon's artillery, concentrating on this point, inflicted heavy losses on the Russians before they succeeded in gaining the other bank of the Alle.

12. During the Seven Years' War, Prussia found herself surrounded by enemies: Saxony and Austria to the south, France to the west, Sweden to the north, and Russia to the east. Frederick II overcame his difficult position by making full use of the advantages which fighting on the "inner line" offers to a highly mobile army led by a commander who does not shrink from taking the initiative: Without waiting to declare war he seized Saxony in 1756. His invasion of Bohemia in 1757 was checked by the Austrians at KOLIN (see note 14) and he had to fall back upon his own territories. From there he advanced with lightning

speed, first into Central Germany to defeat the French at ROSSBACH (see note 5) and from there back to Silesia, where he beat the Austrians at LEUTHEN (see note 1). On August 25, 1758 he defeated the Russians near ZORNDORF. Eventually, however, the numerical superiority of his opponents became too great and Frederick was forced to limit himself to a more defensive strategy, while his tactics remained offensive.

13. Baron Antoine Henri JOMINI (1779-1869), of Swiss origin, entered the French army in 1804 as aide-de-camp to Marshal Ney, and eventually was attached to Napoleon's headquarters. When he did not get the advancement he deserved, he went to Russia in 1813, where he was made a general and became a close associate of Tsar Alexander I. He is famous for his very influential writings on military theory, the chief of which, *Treatise on Grand Military Operations*, was published in 1805. His basic idea concerning strategy was: "To lead the concentrated force of our army to each important point on the theatre of war and there to use these massed forces in such a way that they attack only fractions of the enemy army."

Baron Dietrich Heinrich VON BULOW (1757-1807) had a varied and shiftless career as journalist, businessman, preacher, and soldier. Toward the end of his life he settled down long enough to write a number of works on military theory and strategy, the chief of which was *The Spirit of the New System of War* (1799). Though his restless life did not allow for careful research, his clear and independent mind made him one of the more influential writers on the subject, who established the use of many of our present day military terms. According to Bülow wars were not decided by victories gained on the battle-field, but rather by strategic manoeuvers against the enemy's "lines of operation" (*i.e.*, his system of provisioning). He held that "a corps surrounded by skirmishing infantry is one of the most pitiful objects." Clausewitz opposed the mechanical rigidity of Bülow's strategy, which overlooked completely the significant role played by less tangible moral factors.

14. This statement is only partly true for such battles as Jena, Ulm, Eckmühl, Marengo, and Wagram.

15. In the spring of 1757 FREDERICK the Great invaded Bohemia with three separate armies. Two of these advanced from Saxony (one led by the King himself) and a third from Silesia, under the command of the seventy-two year old Marshal SCHWERIN. The Austrian army under Prince Charles retreated before the invaders and took up a strong position near PRAGUE. Schwerin's army was late in arriving, and when it finally did, the Prussians defeated the Austrians (May 6, 1757), but allowed a large part of the Austrian forces to withdraw. On June 18, Frederick, though

outnumbered, once more attacked the Austrian army, this time under Marshal Daun, near KOLIN. He was thoroughly beaten, largely because of the numerical superiority of the Austrians and the ability and courage of Marshal Daun.

16. WELLINGTON'S CAMPAIGN OF 1810-1811 was part of the Peninsular War (1808-1813) to free Spain and Portugal from the domination of Napoleon. Just as in RUSSIA, during Napoleon's campaign of 1812, the inhabitants of the Peninsula voluntarily destroyed their possessions and stores of supplies, to make provisioning of the enemy impossible and to hasten his defeat. This policy of "scorched earth," as it is called today, was eminently successful in both cases.

17. In the vicinity of ASPERN and Essling, two villages near Vienna, Napoleon suffered a great military defeat on May 21-22, 1809. After winning against the Austrians near Ratisbon (see note 3), he had made his entry into Vienna on May 13th. The enemy's army, under Archduke Charles, had withdrawn to the north bank of the Danube, and Napoleon, in order to attack it, had to cross the river. In a murderous battle Charles defeated the French, who lost one of their ablest leaders, Marshal Lannes. After receiving vast reinforcements, Napoleon attempted another crossing on July 4. This time he was successful, and on July 5-6 he won the battle of WAGRAM, thus terminating Austria's premature war of liberation.

18. During the spring of 1807, Napoleon ordered his Marshal Lefebvre to lay siege to the city of Danzig. The siege, beginning in March, lasted into May. The Russian commander-in-chief, BENNIGSEN, who was stationed in the vicinity, remained passive throughout, even though the capitulation of Danzig gave Napoleon a valuable base and released a number of his troops, which he used to great advantage shortly afterwards in the battle of Friedland (see note 11).

19. See note 17.

20. Louis II de Bourbon, Prince of CONDÉ (1621-86), known as the "Great Condé," started on a brilliant military career in 1640, towards the end of the Thirty Years' War (1618-48). In 1643 he was made commander of the French forces against the Spaniards in northern France and won the decisive victory of Rocroy, which, at the age of 22 established him as one of the great military figures of history.

Albrecht von WALLENSTEIN (1583-1634), a Bohemian nobleman, was one of the outstanding military leaders of the Imperial catholic party during the Thirty Years' War, though his military education, according to Clausewitz' and our own standards, was brief and superficial. He saw two years of armed service (1604-1606) against the Turks and Hungarians, and from 1617 on he was commander of an increasing number of mercenaries (mostly hired at his own expense from a rapidly growing fortune), which he put at the disposal of the Emperor Ferdinand II. (See also note 22.)

Count Alexander SUVOROV (1729-1800) won fame as commander of the Russian forces during Catherine the Great's wars with Turkey (1768-74, 1787-92). In 1799, he was given supreme command over the Italian armies of the Second anti-French Coalition and succeeded in driving the French out of Italy.

21. Andre MASSÉNA, Prince of Essling, a distinguished French General and Marshal during the Revolutionary and Napoleonic Wars. In the spring of 1800, during the war of the Second Coalition, he was ordered by Napoleon to defend the Italian city of GENOA against the Austrians. The latter suddenly attacked, cut his army in two, and forced him to withdraw into the town with his remaining right wing. The Austrian general Ott laid siege to the city, and Masséna kept him occupied by constant sorties. In spite of the growing shortage of food he held out until June 4, enabling Napoleon to win the battle of Marengo.

In 1810 Masséna was made commander-in-chief of a French army of 70,000 invading PORTUGAL to drive the English under Wellington "into the sea." Again he had to pitch his will-power and determination against the terrible enemy of hunger. The British troops withdrew into the interior, leaving behind them a mountainous country bare of provisions. Only one major battle was fought and lost by the French (at Busaco). Most of the French losses of 25,000 men were due to sickness and starvation. It is largely because of Masséna's skillful retreat, that not more troops were lost.

22. During the period of Swedish intervention (1630-1632) in the Thirty Years' War, Albrecht von WALLENSTEIN, the leader of the Catholic and Imperial forces (see note 20) and King GUSTAVUS ADOLPHUS of Sweden occupied positions opposite each other near NUREMBERG in Southern Germany. After Wallenstein had several times refused battle, the Swedes attacked his camp on Sept. 3, 1632. Fighting lasted into the night, inflicting heavy losses on both sides, but Gustavus Adolphus did not succeed in driving out Wallenstein.

23. Near EYLAU in East Prussia, a French army under NAPOLEON and his Marshals Davout and Ney claimed a victory over the Russians, led by BENNIGSEN, on Feb. 8, 1807. The success of both armies changed frequently during battle, due to the various reinforcements they received, and at nightfall neither of them had won a decisive victory; but the French losses exceeded those of the Russians, who had lost more than a third of their men. Bennigsen, however, realizing the exhaustion of his troops and fearing further reinforcement of the French army, withdrew, leaving Napoleon to claim victory.

24. General Gerhard von SCHARNHORST (1755-

1813), known for his reforms of the Prussian army, was a close friend and teacher of Clausewitz'. While still a captain, he participated in the war of the First Coalition against revolutionary France, and was among the heroic defenders of the town of Menin in Flanders. He described his experiences in 1803 in a memorandum entitled *The Defense of the Town of Menin.*

For several days during April, 1794, a force of 2,000 men under General Hammerstein defended the fortified town against the attacks of 20,000 Frenchmen under General Moreau. When Hammerstein's munitions and supplies ran short and the town had gone up in flames, he led his troops in a successful break through the enemy's lines (April 30), losing more than one-fifth of his forces.

A CATALOG OF SELECTED
DOVER BOOKS
IN ALL FIELDS OF INTEREST

A CATALOG OF SELECTED DOVER
BOOKS IN ALL FIELDS OF INTEREST

100 BEST-LOVED POEMS, Edited by Philip Smith. "The Passionate Shepherd to His Love," "Shall I compare thee to a summer's day?" "Death, be not proud," "The Raven," "The Road Not Taken," plus works by Blake, Wordsworth, Byron, Shelley, Keats, many others. 96pp. 5³⁄₁₆ x 8¼. 0-486-28553-7

100 SMALL HOUSES OF THE THIRTIES, Brown-Blodgett Company. Exterior photographs and floor plans for 100 charming structures. Illustrations of models accompanied by descriptions of interiors, color schemes, closet space, and other amenities. 200 illustrations. 112pp. 8⅜ x 11. 0-486-44131-8

1000 TURN-OF-THE-CENTURY HOUSES: With Illustrations and Floor Plans, Herbert C. Chivers. Reproduced from a rare edition, this showcase of homes ranges from cottages and bungalows to sprawling mansions. Each house is meticulously illustrated and accompanied by complete floor plans. 256pp. 9⅜ x 12¼.
0-486-45596-3

101 GREAT AMERICAN POEMS, Edited by The American Poetry & Literacy Project. Rich treasury of verse from the 19th and 20th centuries includes works by Edgar Allan Poe, Robert Frost, Walt Whitman, Langston Hughes, Emily Dickinson, T. S. Eliot, other notables. 96pp. 5³⁄₁₆ x 8¼. 0-486-40158-8

101 GREAT SAMURAI PRINTS, Utagawa Kuniyoshi. Kuniyoshi was a master of the warrior woodblock print — and these 18th-century illustrations represent the pinnacle of his craft. Full-color portraits of renowned Japanese samurais pulse with movement, passion, and remarkably fine detail. 112pp. 8⅜ x 11. 0-486-46523-3

ABC OF BALLET, Janet Grosser. Clearly worded, abundantly illustrated little guide defines basic ballet-related terms: arabesque, battement, pas de chat, relevé, sissonne, many others. Pronunciation guide included. Excellent primer. 48pp. 4³⁄₁₆ x 5¾.
0-486-40871-X

ACCESSORIES OF DRESS: An Illustrated Encyclopedia, Katherine Lester and Bess Viola Oerke. Illustrations of hats, veils, wigs, cravats, shawls, shoes, gloves, and other accessories enhance an engaging commentary that reveals the humor and charm of the many-sided story of accessorized apparel. 644 figures and 59 plates. 608pp. 6⅛ x 9¼.
0-486-43378-1

ADVENTURES OF HUCKLEBERRY FINN, Mark Twain. Join Huck and Jim as their boyhood adventures along the Mississippi River lead them into a world of excitement, danger, and self-discovery. Humorous narrative, lyrical descriptions of the Mississippi valley, and memorable characters. 224pp. 5³⁄₁₆ x 8¼. 0-486-28061-6

ALICE STARMORE'S BOOK OF FAIR ISLE KNITTING, Alice Starmore. A noted designer from the region of Scotland's Fair Isle explores the history and techniques of this distinctive, stranded-color knitting style and provides copious illustrated instructions for 14 original knitwear designs. 208pp. 8⅜ x 10⅞. 0-486-47218-3

A CHRISTMAS CAROL, Charles Dickens. This engrossing tale relates Ebenezer Scrooge's ghostly journeys through Christmases past, present, and future and his ultimate transformation from a harsh and grasping old miser to a charitable and compassionate human being. 80pp. 5³⁄₁₆ x 8¼. 0-486-26865-9

COMMON SENSE, Thomas Paine. First published in January of 1776, this highly influential landmark document clearly and persuasively argued for American separation from Great Britain and paved the way for the Declaration of Independence. 64pp. 5³⁄₁₆ x 8¼. 0-486-29602-4

THE COMPLETE SHORT STORIES OF OSCAR WILDE, Oscar Wilde. Complete texts of "The Happy Prince and Other Tales," "A House of Pomegranates," "Lord Arthur Savile's Crime and Other Stories," "Poems in Prose," and "The Portrait of Mr. W. H." 208pp. 5³⁄₁₆ x 8¼. 0-486-45216-6

COMPLETE SONNETS, William Shakespeare. Over 150 exquisite poems deal with love, friendship, the tyranny of time, beauty's evanescence, death, and other themes in language of remarkable power, precision, and beauty. Glossary of archaic terms. 80pp. 5³⁄₁₆ x 8¼. 0-486-26686-9

THE COUNT OF MONTE CRISTO: Abridged Edition, Alexandre Dumas. Falsely accused of treason, Edmond Dantès is imprisoned in the bleak Chateau d'If. After a hair-raising escape, he launches an elaborate plot to extract a bitter revenge against those who betrayed him. 448pp. 5³⁄₁₆ x 8¼. 0-486-45643-9

CRAFTSMAN BUNGALOWS: Designs from the Pacific Northwest, Yoho & Merritt. This reprint of a rare catalog, showcasing the charming simplicity and cozy style of Craftsman bungalows, is filled with photos of completed homes, plus floor plans and estimated costs. An indispensable resource for architects, historians, and illustrators. 112pp. 10 x 7. 0-486-46875-5

CRAFTSMAN BUNGALOWS: 59 Homes from "The Craftsman," Edited by Gustav Stickley. Best and most attractive designs from Arts and Crafts Movement publication — 1903–1916 — includes sketches, photographs of homes, floor plans, descriptive text. 128pp. 8¼ x 11. 0-486-25829-7

CRIME AND PUNISHMENT, Fyodor Dostoyevsky. Translated by Constance Garnett. Supreme masterpiece tells the story of Raskolnikov, a student tormented by his own thoughts after he murders an old woman. Overwhelmed by guilt and terror, he confesses and goes to prison. 480pp. 5³⁄₁₆ x 8¼. 0-486-41587-2

THE DECLARATION OF INDEPENDENCE AND OTHER GREAT DOCUMENTS OF AMERICAN HISTORY: 1775-1865, Edited by John Grafton. Thirteen compelling and influential documents: Henry's "Give Me Liberty or Give Me Death," Declaration of Independence, The Constitution, Washington's First Inaugural Address, The Monroe Doctrine, The Emancipation Proclamation, Gettysburg Address, more. 64pp. 5³⁄₁₆ x 8¼. 0-486-41124-9

THE DESERT AND THE SOWN: Travels in Palestine and Syria, Gertrude Bell. "The female Lawrence of Arabia," Gertrude Bell wrote captivating, perceptive accounts of her travels in the Middle East. This intriguing narrative, accompanied by 160 photos, traces her 1905 sojourn in Lebanon, Syria, and Palestine. 368pp. 5⅜ x 8½. 0-486-46876-3

A DOLL'S HOUSE, Henrik Ibsen. Ibsen's best-known play displays his genius for realistic prose drama. An expression of women's rights, the play climaxes when the central character, Nora, rejects a smothering marriage and life in "a doll's house." 80pp. 5³⁄₁₆ x 8¼. 0-486-27062-9

HEART OF DARKNESS, Joseph Conrad. Dark allegory of a journey up the Congo River and the narrator's encounter with the mysterious Mr. Kurtz. Masterly blend of adventure, character study, psychological penetration. For many, Conrad's finest, most enigmatic story. 80pp. 5³⁄₁₆ x 8¼. 0-486-26464-5

HENSON AT THE NORTH POLE, Matthew A. Henson. This thrilling memoir by the heroic African-American who was Peary's companion through two decades of Arctic exploration recounts a tale of danger, courage, and determination. "Fascinating and exciting." — *Commonweal.* 128pp. 5⅜ x 8½. 0-486-45472-X

HISTORIC COSTUMES AND HOW TO MAKE THEM, Mary Fernald and E. Shenton. Practical, informative guidebook shows how to create everything from short tunics worn by Saxon men in the fifth century to a lady's bustle dress of the late 1800s. 81 illustrations. 176pp. 5⅜ x 8½. 0-486-44906-8

THE HOUND OF THE BASKERVILLES, Arthur Conan Doyle. A deadly curse in the form of a legendary ferocious beast continues to claim its victims from the Baskerville family until Holmes and Watson intervene. Often called the best detective story ever written. 128pp. 5³⁄₁₆ x 8¼. 0-486-28214-7

THE HOUSE BEHIND THE CEDARS, Charles W. Chesnutt. Originally published in 1900, this groundbreaking novel by a distinguished African-American author recounts the drama of a brother and sister who "pass for white" during the dangerous days of Reconstruction. 208pp. 5⅜ x 8½. 0-486-46144-0

THE HUMAN FIGURE IN MOTION, Eadweard Muybridge. The 4,789 photographs in this definitive selection show the human figure — models almost all undraped — engaged in over 160 different types of action: running, climbing stairs, etc. 390pp. 7⅞ x 10⅝. 0-486-20204-6

THE IMPORTANCE OF BEING EARNEST, Oscar Wilde. Wilde's witty and buoyant comedy of manners, filled with some of literature's most famous epigrams, reprinted from an authoritative British edition. Considered Wilde's most perfect work. 64pp. 5³⁄₁₆ x 8¼. 0-486-26478-5

THE INFERNO, Dante Alighieri. Translated and with notes by Henry Wadsworth Longfellow. The first stop on Dante's famous journey from Hell to Purgatory to Paradise, this 14th-century allegorical poem blends vivid and shocking imagery with graceful lyricism. Translated by the beloved 19th-century poet, Henry Wadsworth Longfellow. 256pp. 5³⁄₁₆ x 8¼. 0-486-44288-8

JANE EYRE, Charlotte Brontë. Written in 1847, *Jane Eyre* tells the tale of an orphan girl's progress from the custody of cruel relatives to an oppressive boarding school and its culmination in a troubled career as a governess. 448pp. 5³⁄₁₆ x 8¼.
0-486-42449-9

JAPANESE WOODBLOCK FLOWER PRINTS, Tanigami Kônan. Extraordinary collection of Japanese woodblock prints by a well-known artist features 120 plates in brilliant color. Realistic images from a rare edition include daffodils, tulips, and other familiar and unusual flowers. 128pp. 11 x 8¼. 0-486-46442-3

JEWELRY MAKING AND DESIGN, Augustus F. Rose and Antonio Cirino. Professional secrets of jewelry making are revealed in a thorough, practical guide. Over 200 illustrations. 306pp. 5⅜ x 8½. 0-486-21750-7

JULIUS CAESAR, William Shakespeare. Great tragedy based on Plutarch's account of the lives of Brutus, Julius Caesar and Mark Antony. Evil plotting, ringing oratory, high tragedy with Shakespeare's incomparable insight, dramatic power. Explanatory footnotes. 96pp. 5³⁄₁₆ x 8¼. 0-486-26876-4

THE RED BADGE OF COURAGE, Stephen Crane. Amid the nightmarish chaos of a Civil War battle, a young soldier discovers courage, humility, and, perhaps, wisdom. Uncanny re-creation of actual combat. Enduring landmark of American fiction. 112pp. 5³⁄₁₆ x 8¼. 0-486-26465-3

RELATIVITY SIMPLY EXPLAINED, Martin Gardner. One of the subject's clearest, most entertaining introductions offers lucid explanations of special and general theories of relativity, gravity, and spacetime, models of the universe, and more. 100 illustrations. 224pp. 5⅜ x 8½. 0-486-29315-7

REMBRANDT DRAWINGS: 116 Masterpieces in Original Color, Rembrandt van Rijn. This deluxe hardcover edition features drawings from throughout the Dutch master's prolific career. Informative captions accompany these beautifully reproduced landscapes, biblical vignettes, figure studies, animal sketches, and portraits. 128pp. 8⅜ x 11. 0-486-46149-1

THE ROAD NOT TAKEN AND OTHER POEMS, Robert Frost. A treasury of Frost's most expressive verse. In addition to the title poem: "An Old Man's Winter Night," "In the Home Stretch," "Meeting and Passing," "Putting in the Seed," many more. All complete and unabridged. 64pp. 5³⁄₁₆ x 8¼. 0-486-27550-7

ROMEO AND JULIET, William Shakespeare. Tragic tale of star-crossed lovers, feuding families and timeless passion contains some of Shakespeare's most beautiful and lyrical love poetry. Complete, unabridged text with explanatory footnotes. 96pp. 5³⁄₁₆ x 8¼. 0-486-27557-4

SANDITON AND THE WATSONS: Austen's Unfinished Novels, Jane Austen. Two tantalizing incomplete stories revisit Austen's customary milieu of courtship and venture into new territory, amid guests at a seaside resort. Both are worth reading for pleasure and study. 112pp. 5⅜ x 8½. 0-486-45793-1

THE SCARLET LETTER, Nathaniel Hawthorne. With stark power and emotional depth, Hawthorne's masterpiece explores sin, guilt, and redemption in a story of adultery in the early days of the Massachusetts Colony. 192pp. 5³⁄₁₆ x 8¼.
0-486-28048-9

THE SEASONS OF AMERICA PAST, Eric Sloane. Seventy-five illustrations depict cider mills and presses, sleds, pumps, stump-pulling equipment, plows, and other elements of America's rural heritage. A section of old recipes and household hints adds additional color. 160pp. 8⅜ x 11. 0-486-44220-9

SELECTED CANTERBURY TALES, Geoffrey Chaucer. Delightful collection includes the General Prologue plus three of the most popular tales: "The Knight's Tale," "The Miller's Prologue and Tale," and "The Wife of Bath's Prologue and Tale." In modern English. 144pp. 5³⁄₁₆ x 8¼. 0-486-28241-4

SELECTED POEMS, Emily Dickinson. Over 100 best-known, best-loved poems by one of America's foremost poets, reprinted from authoritative early editions. No comparable edition at this price. Index of first lines. 64pp. 5³⁄₁₆ x 8¼. 0-486-26466-1

SIDDHARTHA, Hermann Hesse. Classic novel that has inspired generations of seekers. Blending Eastern mysticism and psychoanalysis, Hesse presents a strikingly original view of man and culture and the arduous process of self-discovery, reconciliation, harmony, and peace. 112pp. 5³⁄₁₆ x 8¼. 0-486-40653-9

SKETCHING OUTDOORS, Leonard Richmond. This guide offers beginners step-by-step demonstrations of how to depict clouds, trees, buildings, and other outdoor sights. Explanations of a variety of techniques include shading and constructional drawing. 48pp. 11 x 8¼. 0-486-46922-0